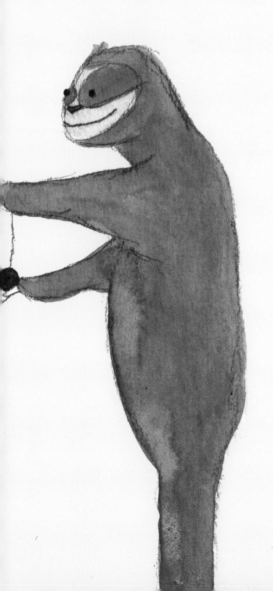

Be
Wild
Be
Free

AMBER FOSSEY

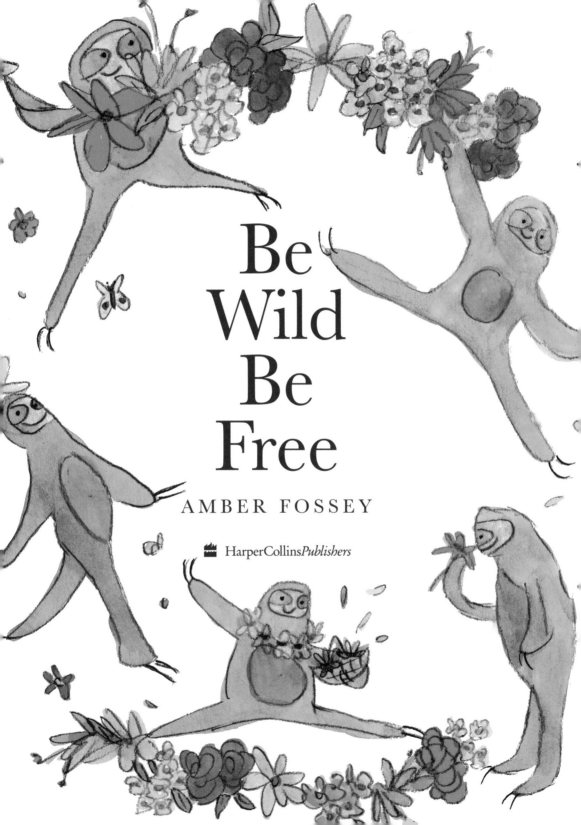

Be
Wild
Be
Free

AMBER FOSSEY

HarperCollins*Publishers*

~Prologue~

oh hallo, friend.

do you hear the beasts
scratching at the door?

they want to be let out,
to be wild and free!

they were sleeping too long,
and now they're
getting feisty.

don't be afraid,
they're pretty
lovely inside.

and never did i see
a more pretty beast
than you.

well now, my pretty beast,
do *you* ever wonder
how to be
wild and free again?

i do.
so naturally,
i asked a sloth.

but he was *busy*.

so he sent me off
to ask his friends.

leopard did not care,
no, not a bit.

he frankly
did not give a shit.

bear could not even remember
where he put his fucks.

so i sat
and looked at rain frog
and rain frog looked at me,
and we realised,
answers don't come easy.

but
one cricket shouting
is louder
than a hundred people
sleeping,

if you listen.

dear heart,
we must creep deeper
into the kingdom of claws,
and listen for
the secrets of the beasts.

come!
we are all in this
together.

you are not
a lone
wolf.

a good place to start
is to follow your toes.
it doesn't matter if you have
two, or three.

(or ten,
if you're a *very* silly creature.)

but if your nose
says no to your toes
and wants to hide
from what's outside,
well it's just fine
to take it slow.

when it gets cloudy
red panda hides
under her octopus hat.

it shelters her
from rainy thoughts
and tickles her into
small smiles.

of all the places
you can go,
your imagination
is as great as any.

reality
is
just

one
way
of
looking
at
things.

see this ant?
he is thinking
incredible things
and dreaming of flying
if he could grow wings.

well, i've seen an ant fly,
it got on a plane.
so i think you'll get high
if you try
just the same.

but beware, beloved!
thinking *too* much
is bad for your thoughts.

most days
beetle packed her bags
and went on a nice little guilt trip,
to see what she had fucked up
the day before.

whisper in my ear
the things that keep you up at night.

together we can stumble from
the darkness to the light.

you see,
this special world
can be a tricky sausage.

every sausage has two ends,
happy
and sad.

a *perfect* life
smells of bullshit.

sloth said he has put
your sad in a bush
over there,
he hopes it won't bother you
for a while.

poor old donkey
has forgotten
what happy feels like,

even in his happy socks.

so donkey called in sick to work,
because his mind was hurting
and he needed to lie down.

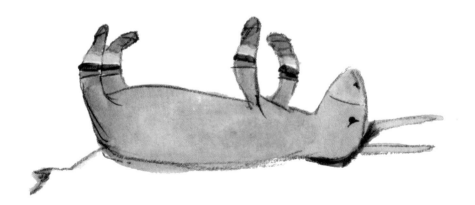

'it all comes,'
said llama,
'of having a weak constitution.'

'it all *comes*,'
frowned donkey,
'of being surrounded by dickheads.'

well, it is true
that in the great dickdom of dickishness,
there are many lieutenants.

'for fuck's sake,'
whispered emu to herself,
after ducking to avoid
yet another
low-flying dickhead.

don't be a dick.

the cake of forgiveness
gets smaller every time
you eat a slice.

it's cool
to be kind.

accepting your flaws
and those of others
can be somewhat
liberating.

there are flies on my wall.

'what's she crying about now?'
they say.

'things that haven't happened yet
but might,'
i say.

the trouble with problems

is there's so

many

of them.

i've got 99 problems,
but my tits aren't one.

where do all the worries come from?

do we find them,

or do they find us?

maybe
we are working
too hard!

snail fucked off early
because he decided
a three-day weekend
would *greatly* increase his lifespan.

maybe we are *too tired?*

sloth slept *so* long
that when he
woke
he found a
sunflower
growing out
of his head.

'a-Ha!'
said sloth,
'it must be spring!'

maybe we are trying too hard
to make
everything
perfect?

manatee stopped trying to please others
with her perfect body,
when what they fell in love with
was her imperfect soul.

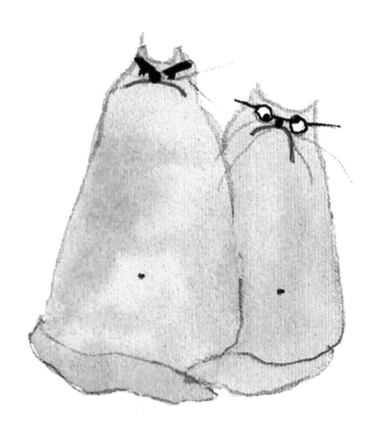

maybe we are
too uptight?

sloth farts
like no-one's listening.

oh *do* let it out!

expressing
emotion
is not a sign
of *weakness*.
it's a sign
you're alive!
and not a
cold,
dead
fish.

i'm pretty fucking cool

and i cry a lot.

what if you're unhappy
and you know it,
and you really want to show it,
should you still clap your hands?

koala is here,
munching on something
green, funky and illuminating;
let's ask him.

well, koala is a *vociferous*
proponent of
a plant-based diet
and mindfulness.

alternatives include
doughnuts
and parties.

this is how
doughnuts are made.

such simple pleasures
are not to be sniffed at.

tapir did not *know*
he was endangered.

so he rose,
snuffled a bit,
sniffled a tad,
huffled much.

at some point,
he ate a banana

he couldn't be sure
what tomorrow held,
but he had survived today!
and that was good.

what a surprise
to be alive!

thanks to
all the heavens
for that.

sloth says
life depends
on which way
you look at it.

by the time tortoise had got
back from the shop,
his damn ice cream had all melted.

he was pleased with his
funky new hat though.

when rat discovered
the life expectancy of a wild rat
was less than a year,
he realised he would never
have a birthday party.
'fuck it!' said rat,
'i'm gonna wear my
spiderman costume
every day!'

life is fucking beautiful!
even when it's not, baby,
even when it's not.

you see,
we are all bananas.

every banana has two ends,
good
and bad.

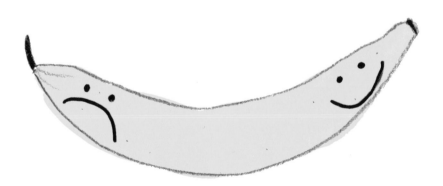

never is
a thing
all bad.

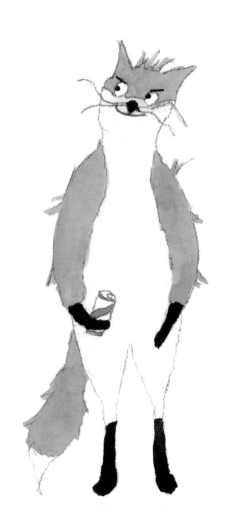

the people were angry
with bee
as he lay there dying.

so they took his honey
to ease the sting
and walked away
with flowers in their hair.

beasts are often
Very Naughty Indeed.

dog does *not* want to sit!
he wants to boogie.

my tits
will not be calmed.

beasts do not like
being trapped.

they like to escape!

so, there's a thing –
humans build a lot of walls.

maybe it's time
we tore some of them down

and *lived* a little.

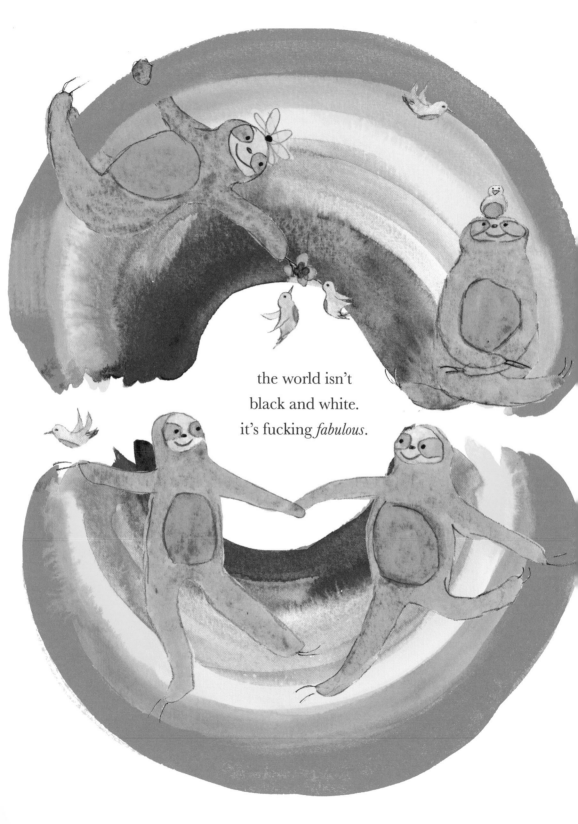

the world isn't
black and white.
it's fucking *fabulous*.

you

are a rainbow.

you were born yellow,
a beam of light,

you cried gaping red,
fought till you went blue
and rode out purple,
waving banners.

you let a black dog in,
shook his paw
and fed him dinner.

you can build
a green den.

you can
heal
a grey king.

your footprints
reflect it all,
like everlasting
puddles.

there's a baby beast
deep inside of you
that never grew up,

and it remembers
things
the rest of us
have forgotten …

like the simple
joy of being alive,

the safe feeling
of being connected,

the wonder
of the infinite,

and how, sometimes,
we need to be held.

when we are small,
it is easier
to believe
in *big* things.

like fairytales
that come true!

some people
told unitort
that he
didn't exist!

some people
are silly.

when we grow big,
we get flummoxed.

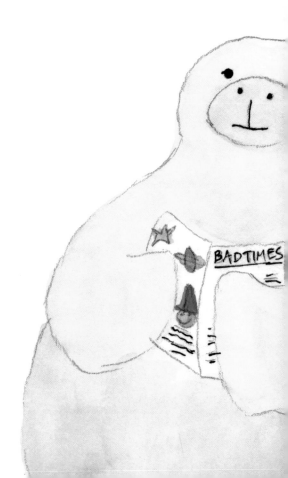

bear has been rowing so long
gently down the stream,
but he doesn't feel merry
and his life is not a dream.

so bear called for help.

because
talking
saves lives.

we can talk about how
you're a bit of alright
in a sea of shite.

we can talk about how
broken things
are beautiful.

a fallen feather
is a treasure,
as perfect lying on the ground
as flying high.

it *looks* like it has broken,
but the power of the feather
is it lifts our eyes
and takes them
to the sky.

don't let the fuckers
get you down,
my love.

remember, flowers
grow from shite,
they just need a little light.

isn't that
fucking lovely.

come what may,
never a day is dull,
my love.

the forecast said
'cloudy with a chance of dickheads'.
so emu put on her dickproof jacket,
kept calm and carried on.

life is *full* of surprises.

i never even dreamt of you,
then there you were!

if you ask a lioness,
they are likely to confess
that beasts do tend to cherish
earth and flesh.

one day cougar looked in the mirror
and realised she was no longer
young and beautiful.

no, she was more than that.
she was majestic.
she was divine.

she was the whispering kiss goodnight
of the dusk to the day.
she was the magnitude of all those
who climbed the mountain.
she was the gift of answers
swept in by the tide.

'i am no longer a princess,'
said cougar.

'i am queen.'

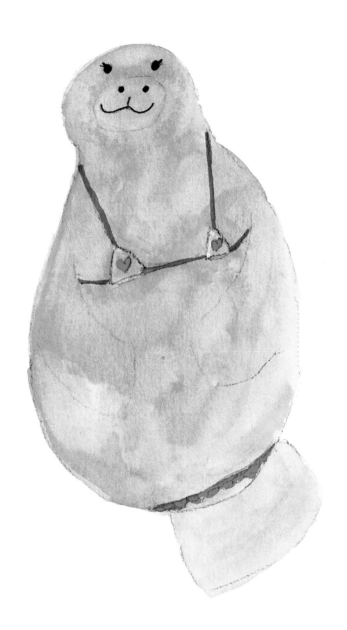

manatee
did not worry about
getting her body
ready for the beach.
instead
she hollered
at the beach,
'are you ready
for ME?'

the sea
lowered his
sunglasses,
smiled and said,
'you betcha, baby.'

every day your body is different
to the day before.
why do we only love it the way
it was one day a long time ago?
or promise to love it
one day that is not to come?
you have had a thousand bodies,
you will have a thousand more.
they all carried your soul.
they will carry it well.

in all of nature,
bodies are *remarkable* things!

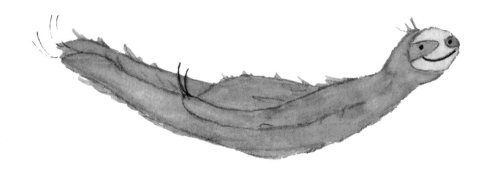

sloths like doing yoga.
that is banana position.

trapped wind position.

dreaming of pizza.

i can do this one.

bear
looked at his tum and thought,
i really ought
to do some sport.

he joined a gym but never went,
so that was money poorly spent.
he tried a diet lollipop
but hunger struck by 12 o'clock.

poor bear was sad,
until he found
that more of him to go around
meant bigger hugs

and *anyway,*
he fucking wanted cake, ok?

beasts are easily *excited.*

have you ever heard anyone say
'quails can't dance in scuba suits'?

no, you have not.

because they can,
and they do.

this cat
is partying
on the inside.

beasts say
do what makes your
heart beat
happy!

stoat spent all his wages
on new jeans.
fuck, thought stoat,
now he could not pay his rent.

but damn, he felt fine
in his fancy jeans.

chameleon was tired of
changing himself to fit in.
'i don't want to *hide* anymore!'
he yelled.
so he turned his camouflage off
and suddenly shone
the most vibrant, dazzling,
magic colours
the world had ever seen.

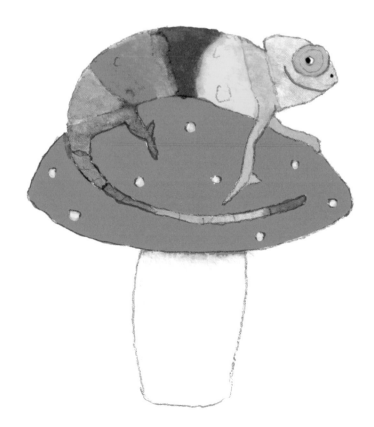

be kinder to your little furry self.

monkey was tired
of seeking affirmation
from virtual likes,
so he quit social media
and made himself a t-shirt instead.

beasts know the key to survival
is to stun every other fucker
with the awesome essence of
YOU

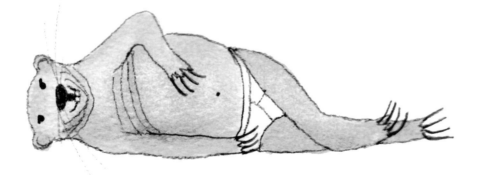

because you are the most lovable thing
my heart has ever seen.

blobfish loved it
when people looked at him
and called him weird.
weird was special, unique,
extraordinary!
he basked in weird,
gobbled it up
and cackled it out even more shiny!
all over the fucking sand!
for boring people to trip over.

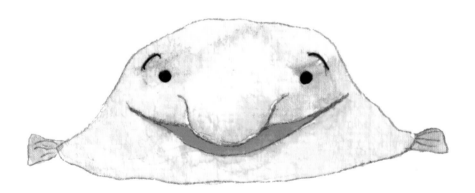

if you're not too sure,
here is a helpful g-raph.

Weirdness

Fantasticness

you are *precious* and must be protected.

well now, friend,
if you're not going to be a dick
when you grow up,
then what the devil *are* you going to be?

'i want to be a sunshine,
i want to be a storm,
i want to be a lover and a friend.
i want to be a hugger,
i want to be a home,
i want to be a laugher
and a brave,'
said baby chimp.

but
the careers advisor
could not find
these in her book.

off you go, small one,
with your big heart.

be brave,
be free.

if you get lost
along the way,
you can always be found.

after waiting rather long,
bear decided,
'i belong to me.'

black dog heard them as they walked past
say, 'too big, too old,
too damaged.'
so still he waited,
patiently,
for someone to accept
the things he
could not
change.

for someone to
stop
and say,
'i choose you.'

they said his waiting was over,
they said he was going home!
his tail was beating as fast as his heart.
they said there would be a nice soft bed
and pats on the head
and *biscuits.*
they said it was ok that he was big, old and damaged.
they said he would be loved.

don't ever
let them
tell you
magic isn't real,
my love.

those lights
they are
so far away,
but every night
they come
back
just for you.

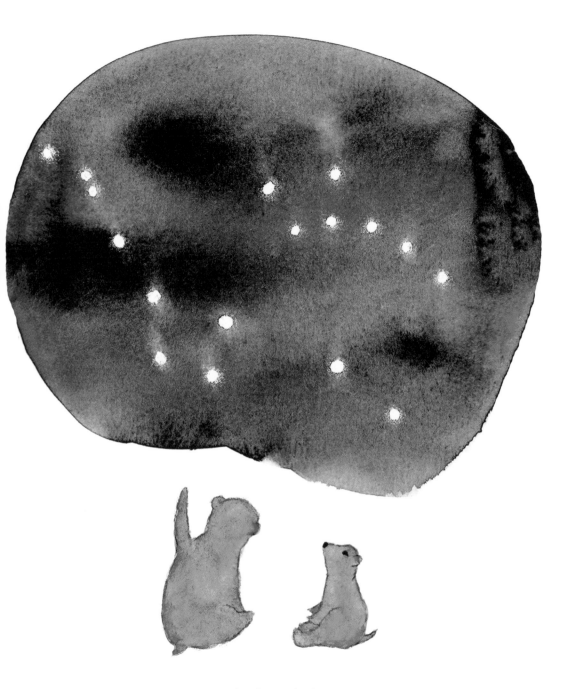

look up, baby,
it's all for you.

wherever you roam,
let them hear you roar.

there *will* be waves.
waves are as sure
as the tides and the moon.

things that make waves
are never forgotten.

'where are you going?'
said the babba
to the old, old elephant.
'i'm going where i can live forever!'
said the old, old elephant,
'in your memories.'

'can i come too?'
said the babba.
'no,' said the old, old elephant.
'you must live here for now,
and make your own.'

old dog was tired now.
his bones had carried him so far,
for so long.
'well done, bones,' said old dog,
as he lay down
and licked them sweetly.

let's meet again, i have to go.
i'll find you where the wild things grow.

sloth didn't know if god was real,
or if there was a big bang,
or if he was just
a fragment of someone's imagination.

but
he had today,
and he had
flowers.

you see, the secret
and the magic
that was in you all along
is that you're not
just a songbird,

you wrote the song.

you're not just a free bird,
you're free to fly.

and you're not
just a wild bird,

you own the sky.

the wild ones
have spoken.
the children of the sea,
the earth,
the sky,
who belong here
as much as you and i.
we share roots,
teeth, flesh,
big beating hearts.
this planet loved us from the start.
all of us,
small souls
dancing under
a billion stars.

and i can tell,
you're just a beast,
like me.

~Epilogue~

there is beauty
in being a human.

with a heart to feel,
a mind to learn
and hands to build
extraordinary things.

you are a gift,
dearly beloved soul,
a child born
unto wilderness.

go forth,
fiercely,
bravely.

kiss the future.

zeppelinmoon

Amber Fossey worked as a doctor in the NHS for 14 years before carving out a new career for herself as an artist. She specialised in forensic psychiatry, working with severely mentally ill offenders in hospitals, prisons and the community. She is driven by a deep-rooted compassion for those that society rejects, mistreats and ignores and for those suffering mental anguish. She believes all souls, human and animal, deserve to be loved and treated as equals. This manifests in her art, where she often champions the unloved, the feared and the endangered. She shares her stories and illustrations on her popular Instagram platform, Zeppelinmoon.

~Acknowledgements~

Let me begin as I started, with the animals.
I am grateful to Mother Earth for her shelter and her jewels,
the best of which walk on four legs, make waves or speak with beaks.
I am grateful to be alive at the same time as her wisest beasts, so that
as a human race we can learn from them.
May we love, respect and protect them all, and raise our children to set them free.

As for people, I am lucky enough to have been helped by some of the very best.
Smallest baby bear and the even smaller baby bobo, you unlocked the cage
and let the beasts out. You gave me everything.
My international bad man, you said I could, but I couldn't have
without your unswervingly patient eyes.
No woman is an island. My mama, my sister, my best girl friends,
all women of fire and laughter and grace, you are my archipelago.
Dad, you drew them all first, wonky pigs and cheery-uppy chumley beasts.
You showed me how powerful a thing is a drawing drawn with love.

Every internet stranger who ever sent me kindness,
I am super grateful for you – you became my friends.

There would be no book without Hannah Dussold who went to the mat for me,
Laura McNeill at Gleam who lifts me up to the sky
and Lydia Good at HarperCollins who made my dream come true.
Huge thanks to all the publishing team at HarperCollins, including
Josie Turner and Hattie Evans for all the energy they invested in *Be Wild, Be Free*.

Dearest beast, don't think I forgot you. You read my book,
and for you I am eternally grateful.

HarperCollins*Publishers*
1 London Bridge Street
London SE1 9GF

www.harpercollins.co.uk

First published by HarperCollins*Publishers* 2020

10 9 8 7 6 5 4 3 2 1

A catalogue record of this book is available from the British Library

ISBN 978-0-00-842298-1

Printed and bound in Latvia

MIX
Paper from
responsible sources
FSC™ C007454

This book is produced from independently certified FSC™ paper
to ensure responsible forest management.

For more information visit: www.harpercollins.co.uk/green

'I am not all these animals, but I aspire to be. I am a little bit of them, and the rest is hope; a universal kind of hope. I want to think and feel like them, without doubt, fear and burden. So I wrote their stories, and in doing so I hope they rub off on me – and you.

Many of these beasts I love came and whispered to me in the middle of the night, when I was feeding a baby or restlessly unslept. I felt them in my bones and never changed a word of their stories. Manatee always makes me cry. When I am angry or upset, the sloths express what I can't say politely, and their silly faces make me laugh.

These creatures are my spiritual guides, and I hope by sharing their messages, you too will aspire to be a little more wild, and a little more free.'

zeppelinmoon